Algorithms

OTHER WORKS BY JOHN ALLMAN

POETRY

Older Than Our Fathers
Lowcountry
Attractions
Loew's Triboro
Inhabited World: New & Selected Poems
Curve Away from Stillness: Science Poems
Scenarios for a Mixed Landscape
Clio's Children
Walking Four Ways in the Wind

FICTION

Descending Fire & Other Stories

Algorithms

John Allman

A ClearSound Book from Quale Press

Grateful acknowledgment is made to the magazines in which some of these prose poems were first published, though the poems may have been cast in a different format: *2River*—"Grackles," "Spare Parts" and "Spraying the Chickens"; *Berkeley Poetry Review*—"When My Sister Lost Her Mind"; *Futurecycle*—"Charon's Oar" and "The Guide"; *Kenyon Review Online* (KRO)—"Algorithms"; *The Innisfree Poetry Journal*—"Attractions," "Black Crows, Mints, Gum, Lucky Strikes," "Crows" and "The Golden Fleece"; *The Long Island Review*—"Pebbles"; *Pivot*—"Evergreens"; *Sentence*—first half of "Waking in Rijeka" (as "Bones") and "Zagreb"; *UCity Review*—"Eileen's Root Canal" and "Quotidian."

Many of the poems first appeared in *Attractions*, a chapbook published by 2River Press. "The Guide" was also chosen by *Verse Daily* for a Weekly Web Feature.

Copyright © 2012 by John Allman

Cover photo: "Large Stone Block Steps Into the Water Near the Olympic Village at False Creek, Vancouver, Canada," courtesy of twobrained.com

ISBN: 978-1-935835-08-0
LCCN: 2012943564

A ClearSound Book from Quale Press
www.quale.com

Contents

Foreword | vii

Did he *intend*?

Algorithms | 3
Attractions | 6
Black Crows, Mints, Gum, Lucky Strikes | 7
Charon's Oar | 8
Crows | 9
Au Cinéma | 10
Drums | 11
Dreams | 12
Eileen's Root Canal | 13
Elegy | 14
Maintenance | 15
Fullness | 16
Evergreens | 17
Grackles | 18
Grain Dust | 19
Grand Jury | 20

Not specified. Not possible. Against all odds.

Le Chant D'Amour | 27
Lula and Ardi's Bones | 28
Lula and the Death of Daddy Longlegs | 29
Lula Takes a Picture | 30
Lula's New Mattress | 31
Lunch | 32

33 | Money
34 | Pebbles
35 | Literary Man
36 | The Shrapnel That Struck Apollinaire
37 | Monday
38 | Siberian Princess
39 | Spare Parts
40 | Quotidian

…the…incoming tide.

43 | The Guide
44 | Croatian Suite
53 | Species
54 | Spraying the Chickens
55 | The Frescoes of Doodletown
56 | The Physical Good, The Moral Good
57 | Two Thousand *Something*
58 | Ruff Collars
59 | The Poem
60 | The Singer
61 | Think of
62 | Throwing Away the Penis
63 | Tomatoes
64 | Watchful Waiting
65 | At My Age
66 | When My Sister Lost Her Mind
67 | Year's End

Foreword

"Not another book of prose poems," my friend said a few months ago, commenting on a recent publication. It's not an uncommon refrain from fifty-something poets who cut their teeth on the genre, attracted to its much bally-hooed subversiveness. There is, of course, some justification for this exasperation. Young poets never realize how difficult it was twenty years ago to have individual prose poems (forget entire collections) published. The implication of the remark's jadedness is that there has been a general watering down of quality, as more and more poets write short prose devoid of freshness of language or surprises of any kind. After all, what could be easier to write than a prose poem?

Although I tend to agree with this judgment, there is also good news. In spite of the mediocrity of the last ten years, I have come across collections of prose poems which are destined to be classics. Although there is very little stylistic or thematic connection between these books, each one seems driven by an idiosyncratic voice. Not some undisciplined primal yawp of a young poet. Certainly anger and disenchantment are present in these books, but they are balanced by years of experience and wisdom. It's as if the prose poem was always waiting for them, and, fortunately for us, they bring all their powers to the task. John Allman's first full collection of prose poems, *Algorithms*, is one of these books.

In *Algorithms*, Allman writes an odd travelogue, comprised of physical journeys to specific places, reflections on his early years in New York City, imaginative trips with Charon the boatman, and notations on his current day-to-day life—all synthesized by a poet trying to make sense of the past in order to prepare for a future, which sometimes isn't pretty. His prose poem "At My Age" demonstrates that not-so-pretty reality so beautifully and honestly.

We can only marvel at the effortless leaps Allman makes between past and present, between precise imagery and subtle abstraction, between the personal and the communal. Moreover, the prose poem seems the proper fit for such a venture because by its very nature it embraces disparate emotional and stylistic leaps, allowing for a kind of controlled distraction.

If Allman is indeed on a journey, the title of this collection becomes a tease. One dictionary defines an algorithm as "a finite set of unambiguous instructions performed in a prescribed sequence to achieve a goal, with a definite beginning, a definite end, and a finite number of steps." Allman's poems, his agenda, is to flee such comfortable precision, instead offering more authentic *algorithms*, ones that don't provide a hell of a lot of consolation or surefire directions to lead us through a series of unpredictable events (life) that often treat us like Charon, who, as in Dante's *Inferno*, uses his oar "to beat the dead to remind them they're dead. And they feel it, the idea of being struck, the shame of it." Indeed, death is both the muse and anti-muse of this book.

The imagination provides a stay against "[t]his nothingness," which Allman realizes, "won't do, this *néant*, this vaguely bad odor drifting into the room." In this sense, *Algorithms* is a guidebook of sorts, suggesting one way for the imagination to assert itself is by doggedly creating and mulling over images, then searching for connections between them. And when that fails, there is always the "kiss," the "unspeakable warmth of thighs." Or as he states later, "[f]or love, words lean together."

Indeed, there's a lot of eroticism in this book, yet another way for us to thumb our noses at fate and death, another way to face the "year's end," not "expecting a dead poet to lead [us] to a flaming river." Like Allman, we're on our own, and forced to ask, "What's real?"

— Peter Johnson

To the Jorge, the Killian, the Kent, the Allman-Coleman, the Statler, the Bolner and the Barbarakis families

Did he *intend?*

Algorithms

Final State

It's not what you did in the third grade exactly—reciting *theory* and *shepherd* letter by letter in the class spelling bee—arriving at wholeness beyond any doubt, or even going backwards in what later you'd call heuristic. As if by being undone all things had their beginning, where everything's reversible. But the newborn cries, the small lungs flutter in the never-before air, the clutched red hands grasp a collapsed idea, an untouchable flow. A mother's milk the taste that appears before the tongue is aware, and what is necessary tends like a first word, the hand wiping the fogged window, the sudden *screel* of car brakes on a cold morning. All this cause. All this shoulder-to-shoulder advance. All this strung language.

Decidability

Of course there must be an object to move toward. Or away from. The sugar bowl on the table, the blood-stained Band-Aid. The bad tooth, the broken crown, the recurring cyst on the lumbar spine. The spiral notebook with no entry since your brother died. Think of the Ouija board, how it takes two unmatched hands, two lives to seek a third, the missing loved one, the long-haired child, the drunken wife, who you must have driven away, while another partnering hand steers always your direction. Lying awake all night doesn't bring you to a zero state. Something is always making itself. Turn down a dark lane, shut off the engine, the last of twilight still burns a hole through clouds, the mawkish music on the local station all but anesthetic, the singer's final word *deny*.

Guessing

Look at the odds. Wear a blindfold, reach for the glass, you'll be close enough. What's a bit of slosh. What's a damp thigh compared to the dry stick always in the dry hand. The same struck surface bruising to the mind's anger to get it right. As if we're here by chance, some peakéd neuron coughing up its DNA, spewing a very odd feeling into being. *Pain. Shuddering joy.* And we move along that edge, fingers trailing along the handrail, the sea below at times too much to resist. Who would know? It's all *might-as-well*. Or *what-the-fuck*. You wouldn't poke a finger in your eye, but that hole in the ground right there where light is coming through, you might whistle down it, take a good long look, lower a string, put your index finger in up to its hilt.

Attractions

You've got to include mosses and ferns. The green dampness. The star anise. The child gathering an armful of black-eyed susans like suns unpeeling themselves. Think of teen-agers taking Ecstasy in the club on Forty-Sixth Street, how the excluded girl's make-up streaks her face outside in the rain. Times also get tough (*time* is easy) for the amoeba, there's famine, no bacteria to eat. One amoeba protrudes to snag another. They ripple into each other. Even Einstein was confused in love. He wanted both his cousin—the mother—and her daughter (such lace around the throat!). Just think of him in Zurich, in a first-class compartment, holding a pungent, skinned orange in his hand, looking at his reflection in the window of a train on the next track pulling away from the station. He doesn't know who is standing still, who is moving. Who first woke to the scent of the other.

Black Crows, Mints, Gum, Lucky Strikes
On the Northway

I expect towns like Famine and Burnt Hills just before Saratoga; the cruise control jerking the Buick forward, pacing the roofing truck blowing a dirty snow of asphalt bits, old tiles piled in back. I flinch when grains strike the windshield, my attention still thin in the gravities of North, the poems read at Clarkson U. Words swirling into the eye like soot. Like boyhood. The more I rub, the worse it gets. Streaked vision. A haggard grin. My father clutching the paper bag filled with Black Crows, mints, gum, Lucky Strikes. In his Memorial Hospital in the middle of Welfare Island, he tilts, and tankers leak past on the East River, the Queensboro Bridge sags a dowager's black lace. Words seep outward from a mildewed wall. His cane grabs an inch of floor and I follow in his wake, and he sways, as if still behind the wheel of his cement truck: the ready-mix of broken youth, too much grit—like that nineteenth-century stuff dug up on the far end of the island; old City Hospital a tumble of gray stones where he was first bedded, doves flown from his vacant mouth: his right hand forever asleep within mine; the driver of the roofing truck all smiles, waving me past.

Charon's Oar

He uses it to beat the dead to remind them they're dead. And they feel it, the idea of being struck, the shame of it, though they have no bodies. They keep turning back up the slope to the security guard, to return through his scanner. Their sins neatly packed years ago into plastic containers out of sight on the moving belt, the music almost too low to hear. They start shouting they left the bathroom water running. An uncut lawn is choking out Grandma's petunias. The guard shows them the scanner screen. Zero. Blank as an x-ray of missing lungs. There's no going back. Now they're really afraid. They expected eternal dolor. A permanent howl. Even the dark lake where they'll swim face down, peering into their gone lives, their loved ones with new lovers, children weeping at a grave. This pain will never cease. But at least it's something. They don't mind Charon beating them on the head — if they have a head. Poking his oar into the middle of a see-through spine. Separating their remembered buttocks. Spinning them around to face each other and wail. Pushed to the leaky end of the boat, fumbling with prayer, fingering their beads, their last words a final cough, it's okay. They're still here, wherever here is. The cold sweat of their souls just a dampness of the air, they think of Broad Creek, the oyster beds, the buzz of twilight diners reading menu specials, the fried clams, the 50-cent peel-and-eat shrimp, even the greasy hush puppies. *How about another beer?* Charon grins. *You schmucks.*

Crows

"Today," she said, "the crows look like Hasidim," and I saw them in the maple, wearing black hats, their long curls like scrolls of text coming loose from their heads. One of them flew to a topmost branch and swayed on the tips of his feet. Another tilted his head and made a chuckling noise in the voice of a robin. She looked out and said, "There's no sense in misery, when juncos share this bounty with cardinals"—the feeder atop its long pole wobbling above the husks of seeds, a mild spongy earth. I saw laborers pushing wheelbarrows, dark bandanas around their necks, sweat trickling down their forearms. A bishop blessed them from his balcony and red buds fell upon his garments. I saw a hawk grooming himself under his wing in the leafless catalpa tree, the sun gleaming on his beak, his nostril-hole a permanent wound. Then everyone flew off at once. "That's the way it is," she said later, her nightgown open, breasts full in the moonlight. I saw a man with chapped lips at her nipples and I burned, oh, how I burned.

Au Cinéma

Why are they driving so fast down a dirt road? A woman tossing in the back seat, her yellow scarf loose around her neck, her lips half parted in protest, the driver bent over the wheel, his greasy hair swung forward—a panel truck pursuing them, something next to him in the front seat that might be a child or a doll still in its cellophane envelope, glitter coming off it possible only because of moonlight. Now a village street, one café open, the green grocer shut, the car speeding past the church with its cemetery, funeral wreaths sprawled on a crumbly grave. It's us in the car, me wiping my eyes, you sitting up, knotting your scarf, our daughter leaning against me half-asleep on the curve. Until we wake in Paris safe again.

Drums

Uptown, across the river, police are gathering for the black youth march. Uptown: barricade pens, cattle chutes, the shimmer of helmets. Uptown, there is too much debt. But in Brooklyn, dreadlocked and tall, he bends over a shimmering steel skin doing Joo-VAY and the pings of Trinidad shimmer down Nostrand Avenue. Corn soup, roti, sorrel-scented beer, lost jobs, lost wives, pursuit and odor of a perfect pitch. Take this to a village on the Black Sea, take this to Golcuk's earthquake, take this to the anchovy casserole lying in the rubble, take this to the ferry from Istanbul arriving to take families away, take this to the open fissures of a land. Take tamboo bamboo, biscuit tins, bottles, scrap-iron-struck triangles vibrating prayer from Brooklyn and be joy.

Dreams

Did I think there were no ethereal parts? That the four-hole Buick parked too far from the curb is really there? That the four-poster bed with a scalloped canopy keeps me in shadow while I twist and turn, believing I'll be late if I don't rise and shine? Look out the window. The Buick's gone. A little garden there, the dew-heavy narcissus shut tight as a book, my name written everywhere inside. Where's the action? Where are the people? This nothingness won't do, this *néant*, this vaguely bad odor drifting into the room. I keep snapping my fingers like a worn-out magician, trying to awaken his life story. Freud eating a Rocky Road sundae, his beard stained with raspberry sauce. Is that blood? Is that you? Are we embracing? Kiss me quick, before we dissolve on the rain-swept streets.

Eileen's Root Canal

Dr. Cohn's/root/canal/office in rear of a quasi-Aztec bunker. E goes in, disappears behind glass partition, white uniforms, smiling women, dentist's basso voice, $50,000 BMW. I'm reading *People* magazine. Teeth, teeth, teeth. Swimming pools. Ads for the Caribbean. Air-conditioning so cold: where in the Virgin Islands: huge hibiscus, rose-colored parchment trumpets, pollen-laden stamens, hyphenated-peeled-back-foreskins: burned odor of tooth enamel triturated by Cohn's drill: where beneath galvanized tin roofs, Johnny cakes and Vi's chicken, all cats on that island the same narrow Abyssinians, as if one and one only; imported mongooses diurnal and wrong for nocturnal rodents: wild donkeys who once carried sugar cane down volcanic slopes: me, sweating and giddy on forest trail to Reef Bay Sugar Plantation, E saying, "Get out of the sun!" I should be in there holding a parasol over her, blocking Cohn's death ray, the garish yellow/green on her face, the miniscule canal and empty tunnel of her tooth's nerve: "There it is! There, there!" The land crab disappearing into its hole, a tarantula, and all the signs saying you can keep the coconuts that fall from trees but please dispose of the shells: *Pang. Pang. Bam.* You could be knocked unconscious. You could have your skull split. You could open your mouth and feel nothing at all.

Elegy

I have it all in my mind, she said. A slippage of opposites. Late ice, early spring. Confusion of black leaves and slush, footprints on the carpet, seasonal death the politics of earth. I know just how it will go, she said. Not the story in today's news, a whole village wiped out for its sympathies. Women tying their infants across their bodies. Birth and destruction. Loss. I know just how it will go, she said. What a fine story, to have been at his mother's knee, honest as the day. Years later publishing others' definitions of love. A fire-proof vault containing all his books. When the lights dim, a woman, any woman like herself in black fish-net stockings knows that wives are forgotten. And children. She takes it to bed every night like a glass globe, his face that shatters on the surface of a pond. A cooling grace, she said. But not silly either. A mist settling on striped Japanese morning glories that crawl up the lattice. She feels them in the tips of her fingers. Mouths opening. Speaking his name.

Maintenance

Time to slam this water-heaved front stoop: sledge-shatter concrete matrix, separate slate, chop out brick stairs. Odors: wet sand, cement dust: first construction 1953, Korean war ending. Every job: "What's your draft status?" Half-bricks and quarter-bricks left over, thrown into sand: the v-angle of rain gutter spilling water: clotted with catalpa pods, asphalt particles from roof tiles, alluvium, silt, drippage onto picture window. *Transcendence*. Stuck on this ground, contact-cemented to earth. Too high now on the ladder, scooping rain gutter, screening pulled up. Ow! Ow! Ow! Wasps! Pinky torn into: honeycombs filled with wriggling larvae. "What's wrong?" Wasps, wasps. Finger. "This is war." Jet-spray slaughter: insecticide infecting nose. Throbbing: Leo's story how he died from hornet sting: no pulse, no breathing, dead in the emergency ward. *Leo now going to inerrant Bible church hearing of the seven-year turbulence before the world ends, half the world dead, judgment, millennium, while he seeks Miriam's soul, which will no longer be Miriam, their fifty-four years rising in the burned-off mist of Mohegan Lake, her chair empty beneath the willow.*

Fullness

...il troppo pieno simula il troppo vuoto — Eugenio Montale

A glass half-full, half-empty—if that's how you half-see, half-miss things. Fullness perpetually open and devouring, a maw, a wet hunger engulfing high-rise buildings, the tenants struggling with rent, the fields they cannot see where you have paused at a river's edge, horses on the other bank with their bent necks, their lips touching water, knowing as they drink there will always be more. Emptiness the blown-into brain of the soldier who looked down at the roadside bomb just below a surface he thought too full to contain anything except itself. And whoever he was at that moment now a lost fullness that will not admit touch or renewal, being so complete, so self-sufficient that children would reach toward him as a prince in a gone fairy tale. His emptiness, if you can call such a thickened sense of light and humid air anything that hollow, his emptiness a silence within each word, so that his spoken *tree* or *horse* or *car* or *you* is each time a complete thought, a finished event, a table set for one, the spoon and fork and knife forever gleaming and unused on a clean white napkin.

Evergreens

Whoever planted these Douglas firs must have known that sixty feet of darkness standing upright under a full moon would gather into itself more than reflection or paleness of age; that so many branches would never splinter to the weight of chickadees, nuthatches, cardinals. They must have known these flung arms would silhouette the spaces of Orion, that unspeakable distances traveled by light would open in our blood like a fever, that I'd stand here in the hollow of a single moment running my finger along the smooth edge of being.

Grackles

Autumn in the biome. Our yard busy with grackles landing around the feeder, their iridescent hoods a stylish variation that clerics strive for, eyes bright, insane, their *crawk* a throat made raw with singing notes too high. They're stabbing yellow zoysia grass, hopping mad, glaring at chipmunks who have scampered under the drooping leaves of hosta lilies. A cardinal in the umbra of dried hydrangea blossoms, his redness the tongue naked to the air, loosened from its proper place in the heat of the mouth. A wet fear works its way among chickadees, titmice and nuthatches, the speckled lone woodpecker clinging to the edge of the feeder. They rise in a black cloud, the grackles, they're done, they break up like flak, bit by bit and all around they fill the dusk with thin lament, and squirrels rush for cover.

Grain Dust
North Dakota

Adjusting Jay's binoculars: blotched sugar beets bouncing out of trucks, squashed like squirrels back home; robins lacking an orange vest, stripped to basic black, piercing a stingy grass, veering among the reeds in Kelly's Slough, half-risen grebes dragging lobate toes. Flatness. Escape. A row of shelterbelt trees fingering the wind. We pass huge fields of sunflowers, their faces drained of oil; road dust rising from phantom bison, air dry as the syllables of taciturn men in coffee shops, towns with one barber shop, a Bible reading-room. Jay steers his dented Dodge and waves at half-boarded buildings last year's stranded motorists tried to reach, leaving their ice-clogged cars, their lips blue. We enter a grain elevator, high walls a combustible dust once slid down from a farmer's chute. Blown. Bankrupt. This land like a Lakota shield spilling light, the Red River swollen each spring; the gnarled branches swinging around, tumbling home.

Grand Jury

Purple Pants

Gets out of the yellow cab on School Street in her red glasses, red blouse, purple pants. Weighing 300 pounds. In her mind inconspicuous. Two hours ago swearing herself to truth, the crossed legs of jurors in swivel chairs—as if everyone wasn't all the time everywhere within the circle of the Almighty's looking, as if He wasn't inside them saying, *write that down*. Five twenties in her purse, a soda straw, driver's license with that other man's last name. Broad as daylight waddling past the furnace cleaner's truck with smudged windows, cops inside camcording the huge progress of her need. Man on the roof spotting birds with cheap 5X binoculars—jerk-necked pigeons, sparrows pecking around the litter of evening love, cold fries, crumpled Bud cans, all the parties she lay down for, kisses tasting sour, the man on the roof writing it in an 89-cent pad. She's breathing hard, reaching the white Lumina. The man behind the wheel, the one they call the Sad Man out on bail, envelopes in his jeans pocket pressed against his groin. Slide her hand in there to feel him? She's hot in her purple pants and red blouse and red glasses, with Him peeking into everyone's private parts—as if His flesh son, the palpable one, pinned her against the tree with a hard-on. Everywhere his animal saliva dripping out of fruits and flowers, that sweetness drying to a powder. His agents secreted in a sooted interior, ogling His streets for transgression, looking at her sitting in the white Lumina holding out three twenties to the Sad Man pulling out two envelopes of dehydrated love, while she is waiting for a little change.

Broken Window

Mother upstairs, her nightgown a meadow, the middle finger of her left hand knobbed and achy as she listens to noise crackling up from the porch door. "It's raccoons," she says, "for bird food," scratching after sunflower seeds in the old cookie container. Can they smell through metal and rust the spicy potpourris in the glass bowl on the dining-room table, that cinnamon-tongued odor drifting under the hall door, under the season that is changing? Father has gone downstairs and Boy Friend is squeezing through the bottom half of the storm door, the plexiglass panel pushed out. Nose-scarred Boy Friend told never to return, smashing Father against the radiator, yelling for money—he needs money—knocks Father through the window. He needs money, he needs money. Where is she, why didn't Daughter his Girl Friend open the door and let him in, how many pills has she taken, sleeping like the dead? Mother halfway down the stairs. Father bleeding. Mother in her nightgown, cold air slipping down into the open neck of her nightgown, a dim light concealing the lovely floral pattern of her nightgown, scuffle and scream and thud against the wall so violent something is tearing at her body inside her nightgown, her seventy-two years. She must go upstairs to the bedroom, put on her robe, cover herself before calling the police, her lips trembling, *imagining being outside on the icy street naked and staring into the house at Boy Friend throwing the pot-pourris against the wall in the dining-room, Father bleeding, no one unlocking the door to let her back in.* Boy Friend crying, why didn't Daughter open the door, how many pills had she taken, sleeping like the dead?

Nickel Bag

Did he *intend* to sell the foil packet to the man going from bar to bar at 4 A.M.? Agree to give up the snowy high with a woman who never showed up? Expect the quarters from a gashed parking meter the man poured into his hand to sound like a jackpot there in the light of the train station so deserted that the two plainclothesmen could hear his congested breathing? He didn't *mean* to feel sorry for the quiver in the other man's speech, the odor of fast-food grease coming off him like the miasma of a dead animal. Did he *really think* the clunk he heard down near the tracks was the last icicle falling in a winter much too long? Did he remember the raspy voice of Mrs. Ramsey next door coming through the wall six months after a difficult birth, saying, "No, no, no, no!"? Did he *wish* to talk so loud about a nickel bag that he *saw* the other man's thick court file opening like a newspaper he could leave for days on the hassock in front of his uncle's tattered armchair before noticing someone he recognized?

He didn't *know his knowing* was the fruit of action when he nodded his head and reached into his pocket, never believing they were not alone, that the heavens beginning to pale in the slow light coming up over the river would not reappear. Yes, he *felt* a tremor in the man's soul when the packet slid from palm to palm like the passing of miles on the slow road from his mother's home in Alabama. But did he *really possess* what he passed on? Did he *signify* his own meaning to the single vapor lamp that suddenly withdrew its pink glow in the early morning? He heard *an echo of himself* in the other man's footsteps ascending to street level. He heard *the law* rushing upon them both. He turned aghast at the face of fear. Of hate. A weapon raised to heart-height. Did he *comprehend* the glistening bore and muzzle of the joy that had got him dressed and down here, the brief tunnel of its force, the sudden crack of its release, his mind dizzily amused?

Bicycle

A tall boy wearing a special forces floppy hat approaches the wire-mesh fence where a boy spins tumblers in the combination lock to free his ten-speed bike from the fence, thumbing cardinal numbers, braced teeth gleaming brighter than anything his father earned in the fields. The tall boy sneers, "That's my bike." The wire-mesh fence casts finely outlined shadows on withered grass, forming the little boxes that physicists use when time is squared on a train going faster and faster, children getting unborn. A woman sits in her SUV, everything she sees moving quickly, the law that breaks momentum slower than the hurt it takes in the order of things to know property is theft. The tall boy punches the fallen owner of the bike in the face. He pulls a chromium bar out of his waistband, raising it over his head like a French accent over an "é." The bike's owner on the ground says, "Ahhh." He says, "Take it!" The woman in the SUV begins screaming. The tall boy rides away on the bike among the numbers stalled at a red light, "q's" and "z's" of license tags the lettered signifiers that jostle each other like eyes that stare, mouths agape, half-raised hands, the stifled "Hey!" The tall boy on the bike leaving the square, adding himself to an open quantity from a system not quite closed—the municipal parking garage—where he now hides his borrowed motion. But the yellow taxi that is not a taxi but an undercover car drives up to the fallen boy and the woman out of breath from screaming, the detective asking where all the glitter is coming from: sun flashing off windshields; the bumpers of city buses lumbering past; the boy raised up on his elbow gagging on the bright blood in his mouth; the shine in the woman's eyes where she imagines her own boys abused. All this loose energy that hasn't shaped itself yet into the closing wound of sky or slow bleeding dawn or the distant rivers a homeless people cross.

Not specified. Not possible. Against all odds.

Le Chant D'Amour
After the painting by Edward Burne-Jones

It's the sheep meadow in Central Park. She's at a little portable organ and her blind daughter is squeezing a toy concertina. The boy friend, lying on his side in stocking feet, cyclist's spandex tights, looks pretty bored, but that's nothing new. "It's sadness," he says. "You always mistake it for lack of interest." She sings, ignoring him, the battery-driven tones humming above the noise of traffic, her hair loose in the acrid zephyr of the breeze, hazel eyes empty, narcotized. Something too painful to surface. She's almost not here at all. The child, who last year had been seeing colors, laughs now at her squeeze box, the wreath of flowers slipping off her head, and she gropes toward her mother's playing. Passersby walk around them, give them a wide berth, where they seem homeless on their blanket, a styrofoam container empty of fries, the mother's singing making the silence between her and the lover obvious.

Each spring he awakens at her side. She fingers the text of her music, plays with one hand—her child lounging in the sun, wearing dark glasses, as if she'd seen the Grail. But he's got the grayness of cheek, the blistered touch of the forbidden. He's sad because longing repeats itself in her monotonous music, her nasal singing, and no matter how often he comes back from cities or describes the unexpected verdure of mountains, or at a shore, the murals in a beach chateau, her eyes are the empty glass of drained goblets and her child asks to feel the curve of his face, the healed ridge of his broken nose. As if each time he is at first unrecognized, then disappointing when he is.

Lula and Ardi's Bones
"Ardi, short for Ardipthecus ramidus, *is the newest fossil skeleton out of Africa…" — New York Times,* October 2, 2009

The past? *I'll give you the past. A second husband's pinch. His roaming eye.* Ardi's breasts must have hung like bags. Didn't her own not-so-little Jordan suck her dry? What could hairy Ardi know about fry pans and unsigned checks for overdue electric bills, when the sun came and went free of charge. *Listen.* Survival: feeling the tidal pull of ligaments when the moon is near. *Small creatures ran into her open hand, a shelter that closed on them until they were eaten raw. The almost-word for food and food itself so closely knit she could taste them in sleep.* The next morning wake nearly satisfied. Something happening in the brain. A bony apartment become too small. Children safe, snuffling in bed, the sound of leaves fluttering in trees. *She knows how wrist swivels and bends, the torque of a tool, the held rock smashed into nut or skull.* If she puts her hand over this photo of a reassembled hand, she feels a quiver. Begins to prickle. Her middle finger starts a slow tapping, a dance, a nervous beat, strange syllables untrapping themselves in her throat.

Lula and the Death of Daddy Longlegs

The circle of its body dried out, sprawled legs brittle as threads of spun sugar. It can't hurt her now. It never could, its two eyes spying a crumb or bit of bacon or dead fly brought to its soft jaws. So good-natured, sitting there on the wall. Or walking down to the cat's dish, dancing on its eight feet. A joy she couldn't understand, not being given to loping movements. Or sitting with a crossword puzzle under a lamp or hiding under logs or rocks or sitting on the heads of geraniums. She won't snap off the legs. Or pulverize its body. Maybe it was sad, the way all subservient beings get melancholy who are accused of biting mothers and children and people in wheel-chairs. But if there's a spider who can make her feverish or nauseous, cause her to tremble in sleep, it's because she's made to be injured, to get sick, to cry at almost nothing. Now she's thinking of someone who never harmed a soul, who came into her kitchen with good intentions and good manners, always eating quietly and wiping his mouth. Politely kissing her neck.

Lula Takes a Picture

Squinting over her thumbnail, adjusting perspective: the Walgreen's one-time-use camera all about volume; a curved horizon kissing uncertain sky; clouds parting into oriels of architecture she looks through to nothingness, but something moving out of the frame, the square view-window. *Something like a soul crossing space so quickly a blue Doppler shifting light escapes all fear of boundary.* Something like a shadow of locusts over the Savannah River at her feet. The hunger of eyes, polished forehead, swollen abdomen, a rictus, tattered formations of cirrus that will not yield rain or block the sun or the fume of the power plant edging a wild-life retreat *Or form like the particular scar between smile and ear, the shredded sneakers, the hand-me-down smoke-pungent sweat shirt, the broken bangle of her wrist.*

Lula's New Mattress

Something shapes itself to her. Someone's spirit drags her into his time. Now the sun outdazzling the peeled whiteness of dead soldiers' eyes is the open window space where her shade has lifted to morning, the crows in the catalpa peering with a knackering gaze. All this mistake where she tosses and turns, backward and forward: the first call to light, darkness falling from her like a skin, as if she arose from a stuffing of leaves and grass, something held together by animal skins. Never mind an inner spring, or linked fabric bags, or coconut fibers, pea shucks, feathers, silk, brocade-tufted covers that button to press exterior into interior. Memory foam. False awakening. Lucid dream. Her mind exploding. Ondine's curse. But no lover's near. Just the gift of delay, the apnea in which she pauses. *The alpha wave's sudden quiet of bird song, the beta wave spindling her into another dying. Delta somnolence, the deep-down always-forgetting as she presses herself into the mystery of being nowhere at all.*

Lunch

McDonald's: man in booth behind us obsessively at his wife, "Got to be black or white, black or white, black or white." In his sixties, in his anger; his wife nodding, her mind shut off, eye looking through the window behind him, traffic on Bedford Rd., the middle turn lane where Chevies wait. Children whooping two tables away: young mothers: half-copies of the *New York Times*: both toilets "Out of Order." *Beeping, beeping*: Home fries done. America engorging salt and grease. America on the run. America: "Help Wanted." "That's what I said, that's exactly what I said. I did." Eileen and I: work to be done—front stoop, lighting fixture, white paint chalking down the brick wall: how many lawns to cut, trees to prune, rain gutters cleared of sludge, epoxy paint on old fridge, dog to walk, cats to feed, Eileen's father over each night in the second year of his loneliness. David arriving on the 15th with one of his children, Petra keeping the other just in case he won't return: wanting him to stay away forever, the children divvied up, her boy friend's syringes tossed in the bathroom wastebasket, poor David tossed out, for what: keeping order. "I told you I would never do that again. I told you." That man, driving Eileen crazy. We move closer to the children. Shrieks. A boy racing up and down the aisle. We plan the day. We plan the next minute and the next. We plan never to stop planning. Swimming at Lake Canopus. Good wine. "I don't want summer ever to end."

Money

It wasn't because he'd lost his job, that's not why she left him. The streets of Marseilles, one knows how they are, the looks, the sad boulangerie, so many others like himself saying their sons have a right to a home-cooked lunch on Sunday, something Provençal that the Americans did not invent. And this euro, the new money, this kiss with the eyes averted, this paper smile — in the suburbs crowded with Arabs and Africans, it will still be a turd in their hands. The rich, even from the abyss, they pluck an egg. What he lifts from nothing is less than nothing, her last touch lingering on his shoulder, removing with itself all the glitter in his children's eyes, all the air in the room. The government promises work. And he reports, ready as a pencil.

Pebbles

The transparent vase has fallen, shattered its neck and flower-etched sides, flung out our pebbles from Itasca, from icy water scooped where the Mississippi begins, where Schoolcraft made his name, Minnesota's roundness feeding into turbulence. A brittle something has split open, its white nougat center a small nebula swelling toward outer darkness. Thinking of Vicksburg, I heft blue-gray embedded with marble or bone, clash in my hand a glacial debris, tiny mineral souls that wash into wild rice marshes. The little etched vase's shivered lengths of milky flowers so thin they cut like syllables of low-down Biloxi singers with braided hair, knocking against barges, plunking holes in oil slick.

Literary Man

1911, Wiener Café, this grumpy guy in Moriz Jung's chromolithograph, slouching on a gorgeous floral banquette, a mood I know, rejections in the side pocket of his outer jacket that is tucked partly behind him, his face stitched from the fabrics of how many late night dips of that pen on the table before him, the ink pot, the blank paper, trousers hiked up to reveal striped socks (stockings? pyjamas?), unlikely bows on his shoes, oh, and the tie spreading left to right, one end slipped beneath his waistcoat that wrinkles across his abdomen, his hair flat across the top of his head, draped over his ears, who sends me this postcard, making such fun?

The Shrapnel That Struck Apollinaire
When man wanted to imitate walking, he created the wheel, which did not resemble a leg. Thus he created surrealism without even knowing it. — from the Preface to *The Breasts of Tiresias*

It was already there before the first hardening of the seer's nipples>>>already whizzing across the fogged space between soldiers' trenches, finding that side of your head where your Polish mother whispered the dust of crumbling amphitheaters, *Je suis féministe et je ne reconnais pas l'autorité de l'homme.* And when you returned from the burnt-out stars, the failed illumination of ghastly faces, it was still in flight>>>its dead mineral eye focused on the unlikeness of all things, invading memory, jagged as a holly leaf and your birth cry in Rome, its fatherless multi-lingual brain still speeding >>> toward you, *après avoir été soldat je veux être artiste,* the coarse whisper of its passage an excited breathing, something nearly sentient, *ennemi de tout ce que j'aime encore*>>>its kiss the first trepanning, the first prophecy from a distant Zanzibar>>> that here in Paris it would dissolve into Spanish flu, a final sickness, you in your last love's arms>>>beneath the speeding constellations.

Monday

"Don't leave me with my father too long." His mother's brain left to science: all of us leaving something: what I saw last week, tiered wasp honeycomb nest someone threw near the road: every creature building future out of itself, making into the void: *transcendence*: how much being in an hour? Inherence/duration; or intent: what we do we are: what we think we do: what others say we do we are: what we summarize we did: who, in retrospect: we do, coalescing: who, accretive: the momentous/event self: momentum/self: what we are the carrying along: the cataract we move toward. Halted by *Do this. Do this.* How we save each other: the must-do, the orderly room, the swept walk, a shirt dripping on the line, the squaring off of wet concrete. Aha, aha. 80# bags of mortar mix, tub of Thoroughseal, days of curing, stepping into the house: new past with old past, muscle hardened from softness, from use, from effort, from will: worried out of the dark, not like a tightly-fitting part: the present always going loose, baggy, opposite to shrunken pants and sweaters we drop into Goodwill bin. Not allegory. Not specified. Not possible. Against all odds.

Siberian Princess

Unfrozen. They strip away your white upper garment and the red lower one, slide their white-gloved hands along your wrinkled thighs, part the fibers of pubic moss that warmed your vacant interior. The horse that shook the harness they buried you with, he's the dust that blows off permafrost. What was held in the curve of your tattooed hand? Perhaps a slave's penis or staff of wheat. A man in pince-nez like Chekhov leans to the reconstructed shimmer of your missing eyes, as if he were trying to remember you in Yalta, before they built the sanitarium. What's left of dream hanging from your waist in the bag of musty cannabis he pokes into.

Spare Parts

They must be good for something, like Homer's ready-cut hexameters, his ox-eyes and winey tide. There were scabs on Achilles' knee that you never heard about, Hamlet's stutter, Ophelia's infected toe. What if when Emma Bovary died, her jaw slack, what oozed out was "servitude, sash, succor"? All the wrong words you'd ever hear at the post office in Rouen. And the poet thinking of the tyrant's cockroach mustache, what if he picked a flea from Natalia's pudendum and said, "grifter, gasp, Garibaldi"? Always somewhere a crunch of tank treads. Why not "stratocumulus"? Ambling across the *noir* screen, a *flaneur* suddenly modern: "Bite me!" Try: "child's rictus," "a joy pineal," the foot that Karloff dragged in *The Tower of London.*

Quotidian

What evidence, this heat: 95 degrees, the dog scratching, chomping her haunch. Ozone creeping up from the city, old lungs wheezing, a yellow rectangle of grass forming over the septic tank. Our old cat fattening up, her thyroid slowed down by tapazole. All these threads, like the spider web hung between the blue spruce and sibling spruce, visible and wet at dawn. The raw day breaking up sleep and sluggish dream, its formed emptiness undone by lists: *flea-dip the dog, pill the cat, cut-grass the lawn, upleap this melancholy, cool-drink words*. Where specificity fails: coffee like sludge, the arc of the eye's whiteness just so many degrees out of round. The latest death, who could save? Death intoxicant. Death redivivus. Death fuck. A child running from the edge of a lake, crying, trenching the white sand, his mother asking, *What? What?* Once, my brother, the boy running along Rockaway Beach: *What? What?* Years later the drug fuel he poured over himself, in himself, the lit match of his anger grinning. *Did you? Did you?* The day's temperature already unbearable. UPS truck chased by the dog. The cat oozing from her right eye, lachrymatory ash. Farewell, brother. Farewell.

...the...incoming tide.

The Guide

And if he spoke from within a quivering flame, his voice a whisper of leaves in the space between time and no-time, the wail of traffic behind him the cries of the lost, my own childhood streaming stories I cannot tell fast enough, their glimmer the coins placed on the eyelids of the dead, the boatman with a long pole thrusting toward the opposite shore where I will explain myself. My guide weeping now, his own family abandoned in a dark wood, his way back to them impeded by wild creatures, dark dreams. So I console him. I take down the sign that says *lasciate ogne speranza*, the bare lintel we stare at, this entrance suddenly before us—a terrible, loud wind in our faces, his cloak rippling behind him, my thin worn jeans the exact shape of my bony legs. Then we face each other, we walk into each other, through a mirroring mist that seemed so material, his hand and mine passing now through all touching like the cries of birds, his eyes peeled back, a dawn, the moon receding, and what I hold, what I lift beyond this wind a fluttering name, a self, the rough bark of palmettos suddenly smooth as driftwood, where I drop to my knees, my guide in my arms, his last breathing filling my lungs, where the sea glistens toward the round horizon and its endless vowel.

Croatian Suite

Waking in Rijeka, Yugoslavia, 1989

We feel foreign and poor, tiny bars of soap, hose shower, a handle coming off the bathroom door, soft gray outline of Krk, your father's island, humped beyond the shipping's smokestacks, masts, aerials, the Jadrolinija ferry's big red star. From the window I'm snapping photos of municipal buildings, arranging shadows in façades, smog swirling from Fiats made in Poland. It's a regular city, people rushing to work, shops opening at 8 A.M., on the wall of a building the same scarlet "fuck you" from the walls of the "D" train in the Bronx, on every wall from Berlin to Belgrade. At breakfast, there's a family curve in the bridge of the nose of the girl pouring sludgy *kafa*, this girl who resembles our daughter. I think of the woman in black approaching us at Rijeka Station, renting rooms, her face lined with the broken lace of doilies, antimacassars. Her voice a darkened parlor. Outside, I snap the entryways of apartment houses, street signs, moving uphill toward the Austro-Hungarian governor's palace, its open-armed rooftop crucifix since 1948 a star. We're stopped by a young soldier, arms crossed, scowling. I say good morning, *"Dobro jutro,"* and we move off. He follows. Now he's saluting men with stars on their caps. A breeze blowing up the coast from Dubrovnik the soot of war.

* * *

"Sehen Sie." A third language working between us, he's pointing at exhibits. We're in the old Palazzo, a maritime and city museum, our gray-haired guide a retired ship's dentist afraid of heights. He can't drive. Can't fly. I'm touching chipped friezes from a tomb, a child's protruding shoulder, hooked implements of ancient farming that still rub calluses on Krk, my palm fitted

to groves in dry wood beneath photos of women sweeping scythes. He leads us into the ex-ballroom, turning right around the staircase. He laughs. He never turns left, never. And laments the absence on this building of the crucifix that once faced the sea. "*Kreuz,*" he says, "*Kreuz,*" spinning on his heels like a dancer, slim, graceful, sweater on his back, sleeves knotted round his neck. Again he tells us he can't fly. "*Petit mal.*" He shrugs, palms up. We decline his offer of coffee in the small apartment he shares with a cat, his wife off to San Francisco. More young soldiers on the street saluting more officers with stars on their caps, his hand sweeping toward the trees, as I snap him in front of a WWI torpedo, the huge rusty cylinder on the lawn, and he's tearful, saying "*meine Stadt. Meine schöne Stadt.*"

Omišalj—Otok Krk

The stink in the air from the petrochemical works blows away into the harbor toward Rijeka. In Omišalj, the old Roman garrison town, we can't walk to one cousin's house without passing another's, without brushing under a fig tree, without seeing an old dog panting on a low roof, without lifting our heads to grow dizzy reading Glagolitic script on the lintel of the church tower. The hotels almost empty, the nightclub that boomed into the night, noisy with Brits and Germans, shut. No one in Europe or America thinks the NATO bombing of Belgrade isn't splintering here, the eye-blue water clear enough for octopus unraveling toward white ankles.

This town so high on its cliff it's easy to throw boulders on the Turks, easy to argue over mother's house left to the oldest son. Brother and sister against brother. The old stable on the hill facing the petroleum loading dock, now a cousin's house and terrace, a kitchen with cream pastries, a garden hung with tomatoes, a shed boarded up, grandpa's old cart inside. Miljenko has caught St. Peter's fish, mullet, *lignja*, and spreads out their pictures in a book, even as we eat. Back along the path, a cousin has closed the shutters of his house. Not to see us. Not to fume.

Homecoming

The bell tower's script half-Cyrillic, half-hieroglyph, lost speech chiseled above the door, something he almost couldn't say stepping off the plane. Inside the church, the very seat father rose from in 1920 — so many men departing, a field's fibers clinging to their pants, father's cracked smile dry as the land, while mother waved and cried. *Your older brother came first to America but his sponsor did not appear. They sent him back, to an Austrian trench, the gas, the yellow mist, the jagged verbs entering his lungs. He tried the USA again, with you. This time, the doctors sent him back. Gaunt. Coughing up shreds of empire.*

He's in Omišalj, the plaza, boys chased for playing soccer, the church with worn marble threshold that was being stepped on when Constantinople fell. Old as an Illyrian psalm, portico, he's bent like his brother Nikola, dead last May, the same leached spine, the same freckled hands. *You worked nights in Horn & Hardart feeling the warm bread, muffins, turnovers, the last of childhood. A wife back in the village drowning herself because your cousin who never sent for her lived with another woman two blocks from the Hudson River. That flow you couldn't understand.*

Of his mother little is said. Eyes fill. He shakes his head, saying his youngest daughter walks like her. On the patio that was once a stable, sister-in-law shows him the lambskin dress that mother's mother wore; a waist so small, the women laugh, holding it against their broad bodies. His wife not here, her different word for bread caught in his throat, her absence rising with the moon, a chill light, a nephew mumbling, still back in 1944, the Nazi grenade. *Your wife wrote every year, enclosing Christmas checks. They laughed if she used "what" with the vowels from the East, from across the Sava, out of her mother's mouth. Her letters to them like golden threads, while the petrochemical plant seeped acrid odors across the bay. She had such a way of saying you were not just a baker but a husband. A father. A man who could not afford to go back.*

Opatija

On the Kvarner Gulf, standing on the Lunga Mare, the promenade of Opatija, looking west at Krk, in a haze—industrial stacks and shipyards of Rijeka—to the right the humped silhouette of the island Cres—water skier cleaving the water—parachutists swaying down with their rectangular chutes onto the target pad at the Slatina—German tourist snorkeling off the rocks in front of our hotel—the flaking mustard-colored walls of nineteenth-century Austrian villas—the Park Angelina, the Villa Angelina built and named for a beautiful dead wife—venerable pines, the knot garden and grounds tended by young women in white polo shirts and green pants—motorbike shrieking up Maršala Tita—green flame tapering cypresses—fishing boats that glide like a breath along the gleaming water—the hills sloping down to Sveta Marija church—an observatory dome behind it—the row of green hills showing the shape of ancient lava flow now like vast knuckles and fingers with spaces between. The loosened grip of old empire.

The Golden Fleece—Pula

A triumphal arch, an ancient church, but long before that, Medea prayed all night here, thinking the sunset a fleece. Her brother's blood smeared across the sky. His men in pursuit. These meat patties we're eating at a sidewalk café taste of remorse. Betrayed polis. But no one is chasing us, no one afraid to turn back, a crane swinging out over the blue harbor to hook onto a cargo of refrigerators from Slovenia. Opposite us the clerk in the Wechsel window yelling at an Asian man who stumbles through English as through a thicket. That's what happened to Medea's pursuers—turning on strangers, where they were strangers themselves. The vengeful twitch Dante felt in his cheek when he walked through here—expelled from his city—now only the last reverberation of a water truck sprinkling cobbled streets.

Rovinj

The campanile of St. Euphemia on its hill. She's there on top turning in the wind trying not to remember the lions in Chalcedon who refused to taste her perfect limbs, though the Romans broke her on the wheel, the wheel she shoulders up there. Who can say how her marble coffin floated all the way from Constantinople, spinning round and round, arriving here. A miracle applied wet in this fresco next to her sarcophagus. Birds steer to follow her extended hand, toward the island of St. Katherine, the old quarry that yielded stones for the Roman amphitheater in Pula, the stones the Venetians robbed to build St. Mark's in the economy of suffocated gods. All prices in Deutsche marks, signs in Croatian and Italian. A history that sifts, colored and framed, sold from easels lining the sea wall. Ten minutes by shuttle boat, Red Island steeped in the teal shallows of a naturist beach, nude tourists inhaling sweet laurel and myrtle. The green of Aleppo pines shimmering in the distance. An old abbey crumbling darkly behind us, the smell of lost documents. Ancient gulls tilting in the sainted breeze, hooting, cawing like nowhere else, as we hoist a ruby wine to those of us still wrapped around our bones.

Zagreb

This square with its banks of flowers and underground passage to the urine tunnels of pan-handlers and dope-needlers, this *trg* that overflowed with well-dressed patrons in 1927, when a king ruled, this is the place we walk through, nodding at the slit-eyed policeman not yet aware what he will do if elections are nullified next month, his truncheon raised in the street. We amble past old men on benches along a park. They lean against each other, squabbling about Belgrade, this minute being rubbled by NATO. They are unaware that 30 miles north in the caves of Krapina, Neanderthal bones show evidence of benign tumors, the surgical amputation of a hand, some bones bent by osteoarthritis, a people who arose stiff in the dawn. One skull showing a fracture in the occipital bone where it was struck by a blunt instrument in that cave where no one could buy an ice cream from a stand and lick his way through the temporary sweetness of the evening, chocolate smear on his lips.

The Bridge of Sighs—Venice

He sent them this way, the Doge, cupping his chin, waving them toward this darkness already a prison; where shackles hung, an outlined empty space voluble as the one covered by black cloth among portraits of the Doges: "This is the place of Marino Faliero, beheaded for his crimes." This bridge so baroque seen from Ponte della Paglia, we imagined the interior of cake. The Moor swinging his hammer into rust on the bell of the clock tower, all that sound outside, the campanile's golden angel severe in such resonance he moved the Adriatic back. Prisoners traipsed up dank stairs from below the water line.

You back against the steel-braced door, unable to breathe. You know them, the spirits sidling along the broken mortar, hunched and chained in Quonset stone cylinders, dragged here from Dalmatia, who fought to save their trees bundled under water to raise this city. Your people led down the gangway onto the Riva degli Schiavoni; someone who threw rocks from the cliffs of Omišalj, the moles on his back identical to your father's, the blue of your eyes a blueness along his cold lips, your lungs burning with claustrophobic fire, cords straining in your neck. From these stone walls the odor and exhalations of a people, their children hundreds of years later Thomas Mann said wore a flutter of rags.

Species

Across the bay off Mount Desert Island, or at Cross Island, or in Blue Hill Bay, anywhere at all beyond dehydration, beyond cholera, beyond mountains, oxygen thinning, slipping through the gills of caged salmon. Song flat as up-staring flounder. Grouper, snapper, tuna, shark, swordfish, penaeid shrimp, stone crab, blue crab, golden crab, oyster, calico scallop, clam. There's WhaleNet and the size of tilapia. Indian carp and milk fish. The oldest men at Cedar Key sitting on a sea-log bench, that twinkle in their eyes. Listen to their breathing. Shout your name.

Spraying the Chickens

It wasn't necessary back when the hen kept her chicks close and they pecked at her fecal droppings and they swallowed just the right kind of mother love, a touch of illness, a taste of their own blood, and they trembled in sleep. Those days you could eat them without a care. Maybe even find a dark spot near the pimply shoulder, a piece of quill, the memory of a certain kind of flapping. The farmer's wife wiped her hands on her apron after she put the naked thing in the oven and she wiped the dirt off unpeeled potatoes but kept the dusty look and cut the bread. You were so happy and hungry you wanted to kiss her hands that kept layer upon layer of so much world intact. And if something of that got into your mouth, it was proof against the evil to come, the corruption of bodies. The cold touch of strangers.

The Frescoes of Doodletown

Conservancy Meeting on Bear Mountain, before the hike to Doodletown, the 1777 Trail: speaker on the dais hip-hopping a sniper's laser dot over topographical maps. A river sinks out of sight. Ponds choke on algae. A spotted aberration in frogs from too-affluent water. Sun tearing off ozone's silk. The paddle-fish without eyes, its snout crackling with news, every creature homing back to birth, twisting toward the Sargasso Sea. Eileen is talking to Dixie Lee, the retired prison guard back from Nepal with a Sherpa grin. An older couple weary of CNN. The widow with a fruit platter that she passes around. The city far away slurping cool mountain springs, sweet dark cola, heavy minerals leaching into our mouths.

Walking across the great lawn, stepping around turds of Canada geese, onto the old bridle path—we find a family cemetery's washed limestones where mothers coughed up their lungs and buried infants, redcoats tramped single file to Fort Montgomery like a species of fox. A recent grave, the last of the Loves. Downhill, off Doodletown Road, the color of iron trapped in bog that birthed hinges, hooks, heads of hammers, rims of wagon wheels, latches of a door. We're looking for the password stolen by a slave who sold berries to the British, the white paper pinned to each Colonial cap to mark it in the night. Looking for teeth, musket balls, the halloos of sentries up and down the highlands. The walls that pictured their return home, the frescoes with tinted smiles imbued into fresh plaster, the wide-eyed faces looking up from dinner.

The Physical Good, The Moral Good

The old ones did what they could, hacking their way down a peninsula. Burning ships. Grabbing a fleece. Holding off thousands at a narrow mountain pass. Someone hauls up *kalo k'agathia* from the depths of the Aegean—a perfectly muscled young man raising his arm through weeds, a salute to the gods, to virtue's amphora. I'm pictured there, arm half-raised, a collapsed lung, the past trying to re-inflate. Was it you holding a lantern to the sky? Here's wisdom's spittoon, low down, our feet on the brass rail at a bikers bar: something *vrooming* (Florida, a small town near Jupiter). I'm bearded, quaffing beaker after beaker: all this goodness, the smell of marijuana sweet as the breath of the goddess, your eyes the only light a dead warrior might follow to the boatman.

Two Thousand *Something*

This is about the woman who felt God breathing on her as a friend talked about dying, *meanwhile a sun much smaller than ours, with a water planet in orbit, its surface temperature twice what makes water boil on earth, a world in perpetual fog* a wife going deeper into the Congo forest to gather wood for her stove, the soldiers who hold a gun to her throat as they rape her, *the tomb of Alexander the Great still undiscovered though that fresco of a hunter must be him.* This is about bad lungs, tumors on the liver, the girl's remains finally identified after 20 years under a rose bush, the car rushing toward the barrier, its driver's face the first thing to be blown away. *This is about prayers that are pills in a bottle that must be kept away from moisture, the expiration date rubbed off, a child's cry trapped inside the cap.* This is about how good I feel as palmetto fronds stab the air with green findings, Spanish moss swaying in live oaks, the resurrection fern crawling day by day along thick curved trunks, as I free the chameleon trapped between the sliding screen door and the glass door, *as I watch its wounded slither on the creamy deck in a blazing twilight that is leaving red spots in my vision because I can't stop looking at a setting sun.*

Ruff Collars

The *Santa Maria* taking froth along her wormy bow, her swaying fore and aft castles, a pennant streaming like Isabella's sleeves, the tufts of hair above his ears, his swollen eyelids curved and shadowy as the small breasts of Indian women. I mean Cuba not Cipangu or Cathay. *This western half of the world is like the half of a very round pear, having a raised projection for a stalk, or like a… nipple on a round ball.* Because it comes down to the beauty of white ruff collars the six Spaniards (delete the Genoan and make it five) wear like bleached starfish, their lacy points true admonitions to bone arrowheads. I mean bows, satin bows in Renaissance hats, turned-up brims, the peeled look of men's legs between garters and boots, their utter blankness, the little white *INRI* pinned to the vertical beam of a processional crucifix carried by the monk at the rear, sailors tinkling falcons' bells.

Open sewage, cracked syntax, cholera, the Orinoco thrashing like Charybdis, lice implicit in shades of purple beneath a parrot's wing. *There are great indications of this being the terrestrial paradise.* I mean myself, waking in Katonah to the odor of blood, the dogwood bright with dirty linen bloom. Vines hung from mangrove trees like elongated tears, bald Arawaks pearl-fishing off Margarita, and the shackles on his scuffed ankles, his red-rimmed eyes, Bobadilla bringing him home in chains. I mean thin brown arms of girls bought like farms for a hundred castellanos. The cacique Guacanagarix with his men in ceremonial approach, their arms lifted like sleepwalkers. La Navidad's fort rising in the moonlight as quickly as a tin shed from Sears.

The Poem

Study Renaissance poetry, lose the fear of death:
miniature deer with jeweled collars
leaping toward the moon and the queen exposing
her bosom.
—Marvin Sicherman

Staples that knit his chest together over a by-passed heart—small knuckles warming in the sun. His blood no longer fed by the narrowest meanings. This year alone, his sister has died three times in Haifa. That crush of blossoms so near the evening tide, that ruffed white throat. She turned away last visit, ashamed to see him. He turns pages on the long flight home. The moon, always the moon.

For love, words lean together. For this, he reads on. One daughter pulsing through e-mail this very minute. Another paying tariff in the shadows of Parliament, the stamps on her envelopes depicting the river and the punting that strained Lord Essex in the wrist. Her salutations late but sincere. But so many climbed the wet steps from the Thames in a perfect pentameter up to the landing, to the Tower, so many lost their heads, the extended hand kissed.

Speaking Yiddish, dressed in black, his parents always avoided passing the church. "Christians are not good to us." He thinks of the Jews who converted to Christ with their dying breath, their sonorous song lost in the light that breaks into quatrains, the sonnet without its ending, the coupling, the linking, the enjambment, the crowding of the damned to come. He feels a dusty, coarse fabric in his hands. The Queen sitting out there in the audience, in front of the curtain. A loutish rabble shouting, "Author, author!" The lopping off of syllables. The writhing of a perfect last line without its head.

The Singer

He's dancing in the street, chanting his poems, waving a claw hammer, the towel wrapped around him like a prayer shawl. The police are on their way. All the neighbors think about is how many bags of marijuana are in his basement room, how he studied the ancient secrets in Safad, while the great tenors sang in Berlin for taxes. His poems sound like a flute above the traffic, causing injuries to passersby in heart, lungs, liver, intestines. An opinion falls out of a sergeant's brain. The police are almost here. Young Netyana sits on a stoop and weeps for him, her beloved, the stone beneath her thighs ancient as Pangaea, the origin of the world. In his poems, volcanic heat, water, ice. His blunt hammer flattens the air and the city is deformed. The police are dizzy and have lost their way. Inside the car driving past is a tether holding a child in place. Inside the tether is the fiber from which he weaves the poem. Inside the fiber are the 2,000 memories of the first dawn.

Think of

antinomies. Space revolving like a struck musical triangle. Or collapsing into silence. There's always roiling gas. The notion of water. A kind of swimming before there is anything to swim in. A vacuole. A mouth. Movement to any kind of thinking, *irritating*—which is what life is, *annoyed*. An implement pricks you and you bleed. Love tears out your soul (let's call it that, call it anything)—you are a scooped-out melon, an empty deer carcass hanging from a tree, the eye socket without an eye—the wind smashing through stiff palmetto fronds. A kind of clacking in the distance that is mimicked in late winter vegetation, where the usual sun lavishes warmth, the cardinal's perfectly square black face at a tilt as it studies the tossed seed on a deck. And you bring a hand to your face that has just been touched by a wisp, a moist plant or animal filament like the remote mitochondria adrift in every cell of your body, if you even have a body, if this is not a dream from which you will never ever awake.

Throwing Away the Penis

It would boomerang, of course, slicing off the heads of trees on its way back, spotted towhees and nightingales fluttering out of the way. Women filling their cars at self-service gas stations would be whistling and waving, a sound like the single engine of a Piper Cub thrumming over the parking lots of bachelor apartments. It would continue into the dreams of naked consorts tangled in starched sheets, the open window letting in too much breeze, goose flesh beginning along the arms, down into the groin, with the tinkling outside of racing bikes—women in tights, men with insectoid helmets, everyone leaning back to drink from their water bottles, lips wet, still slightly chapped. A gasp, a sigh, perhaps a moan. Something in the air like a detached sound track, a digital glimpse of torpedoes burrowing toward the smooth side of a ship. A flashback of swimming spermatozoa nuzzling an egg. But it bursts out of the tide, it's back in the air, a garish sun drying every inch of it as it speeds toward home—the vacancy of lost laughter, the unspeakable warmth of thighs that open like the receptacle of this song.

Tomatoes

As if there weren't some little piece of unradiated something still floating around just behind the esophagus that keeps swallowing tasteless vegetables from an aluminum tray. His friend the other side of a plastic curtain, speaking through the flap, his nicotine breath carrying fire. The blinking red eye in the hallway signaling someone else going down. Something in the air—if you can call it air—like the Caribbean, a bluish-green he looks through. It's here, seems to be here. The face mask he spat on to prevent fogging now clear as he looks at intricacies like coral that injure a swimmer, looking into himself at the slow gulping jaws of someone so long under he might just as well scrape deeper into a sandy bottom and hide there. Lungs hissing beneath tons of sunlight. He's only checking it out. He's going to pop up gasping, his daughters there in the shade under the sea-grapes, sting of water in his eyes. Sudden noise of an outboard motor and lens of blazing sun all the evidence he needs that he's in the resort bay, a cold current beneath him, the rattling of tubes and wires a fisherman's net slapping against the boat. He can wade out of this and buy t-shirts in the equipment store, the ones with an embossed map showing just where he is, sheltered from the path of cruise ships, the mountains behind him terraced into small farms. A man up there gathering early tomatoes. A wife in hospital whites patting his face dry.

Watchful Waiting
apologies to Samuel Barber and his opera Vanessa

Think of Olivia at the ball, pregnant with Antone's baby unbeknownst to anyone, even the drunken doctor about to announce Antone's engagement to Arianne, who has just finished an aria that almost pledges her fidelity, almost strokes Antone as she would a child. He's so full of himself, but uneasy, seeing Olivia outside the French doors, Olivia looking in, the weather frigid enough to abort any fetus, her hair coming loose, as if she'd been washing stairs or bending over for the master in the library she'd just finished cleaning. Think *hyperplasia. Focally complex.* Say *fibroids. Sonogram. Vaginal laparoscopy.* Listen to the dim gurgle in Olivia's womb. Her soul's eyelash unstuck and teasing one word after another out of what she almost sees. That bitch Arianne with a big ass and skinny ankles coming down the spiral stairs, slipping on her own lies, she's tumbling onto a broken champagne glass, a single jagged finger puncturing her empty uterus. The teeth of the wailing chorus showing all that white as if they were smiling. A nightingale choking somewhere the other side of the river. A mewling regurgitative sound. A tube sucking air, a nurse's *ahem*, the sudden opening of a drain. Antone's tongue swabbing the inside of Olivia's mouth. The chorus outside in the parking lot waving their validated tickets.

At My Age

Wisdom. Biopsies. Grandchildren. Friends crossing over. You think this is easy? Pick a card, any card—the King of Diamonds, his blood-red grin, those eyes like sunsets over the Caribbean. Remember the ferry to Tortola, a sparkling middle-age lost somewhere in the tourist observatory, the stars moving away from each other like the memory of a mother's voice. The world nonfat, nonEucharistic, nonpraiseworthy, nonorgiastic, nonpolitical, something always pulling back the blanket, your chilled feet the two parts of a syllogism that can't get to a conclusion. This is where you cry into a towel, this is where the x-ray technician wears sequined glasses, the music pounding. Palmetto berries fall like shrunken blueberries, today's sea neither unruly nor unkind, a long winter made penetrant by the shouts of children. Brown spots on the backs of your hands where angels have kissed so politely, so feathery in their thoughts, so willing to bow and scrape their wings, so confident in their announcement. At the beach, dolphins are making circles in salt, sun glinting on glossy backs, darkness below. Ah, the hordes, the silvery contact and slide of scaled bodies, the watery lungs that sleep and dream. The moon's cold white glance, the lisping incoming tide. The kiss.

When My Sister Lost Her Mind

1939, *a common year beginning with a Sunday*, the battleship Schleswig-Holstein bombarding the Westerplatte, the Wehrmacht crossing Poland's border, *something already born within you as you came forth*. This the time of dark eyes and olive skin. A history going wrong before the first suckle, *a sister before you not lasting two weeks.* This moment where a chronology might have stopped, a world snapping and withdrawing like a surgical glove. Night terrors just a toothache, a bad meal, a movie about a strangler. You stood at the kitchen window, looking down into the alleyway, but still asleep, still hearing a vast water behind you. *A slow wave rising, roiling, vaguely volcanic—swelling into the loud shattering of a gene: inheritance flowing the wrong way in father's blood.* Did it matter what you did for a living, to live? Transcribing names in the Author's Guild, while your own was slipping away, electro-shocked back into temporary brightness. Days of white walls. The white gowns a fashion show of angels. Laughter of friends you kept in a locket. The one boy friend riding forever on the G train trying to find you.

Year's End

It's not like being in a dark wood or going into a valley of leopards, expecting a dead poet to lead you to the flaming river and the cries of your enemies. Time and travel the same thing, where you get to being where you began, where you thought to go, heaven buckling like the tin ceiling in a play. Think of the rose bending to its root—that old song of self, that old man still preening in the mirrored room: so many ways of seeing who you were, who you forgot to be, who whistled himself down a narrow road, the evening star breaking through a cloud cover as phony as a magazine ad. What's real? The hand at your mouth, your pulse this minute skipping a beat. The cataracted eye, the blur of traffic. The sudden ring of the phone—a lover calling again. Leaves of the live oak falling into the lagoon where a night heron skims the reflection of the moon.

quale [kwa-lay]: *Eng.* n 1. A property (such as hardness) considered apart from things that have that property. 2. A property that is experienced as distinct from any source it may have in a physical object. *Ital.* pron.a. 1. Which, what. 2. Who. 3. Some. 4. As, just as.

www.ingramcontent.com/pod-product-compliance
Lightning Source LLC
Chambersburg PA
CBHW031209090426
42736CB00009B/849